THE DAMON MEMORIAL

84, Charing Cross Road

84, CHARING CROSS ROAD

by Helene Hanff

Grossman Publishers, New York, 1970

F. P. D.
In Memoriam

84, Charing Cross Road

14 East 95th St.
New York City

October 5, 1949

Marks & Co.
84, Charing Cross Road
London, W.C. 2
England

Gentlemen:

Your ad in the Saturday Review of Literature says that you specialize in out-of-print books. The phrase "antiquarian booksellers" scares me somewhat, as I equate "antique" with expensive. I am a poor writer with an antiquarian taste in books and all the things I want are impossible to get over here except in very expensive rare editions, or in Barnes & Noble's grimy, marked-up schoolboy copies.

I enclose a list of my most pressing problems. If you have clean secondhand copies of any of the books on the list, for no more than $5.00 each, will you consider this a purchase order and send them to me?

Very truly yours,

Helene Hanff
(Miss) Helene Hanff

84, Charing Cross Road
London, W.C. 2

25th October, 1949

Miss Helene Hanff
14 East 95th Street
New York 28, New York
U.S.A.

Dear Madam,

In reply to your letter of October 5th, we have managed to clear up two thirds of your problem. The three Hazlitt essays you want are contained in the Nonesuch Press edition of his Selected Essays and the Stevenson is found in Virginibus Puerisque. We are sending nice copies of both these by Book Post and we trust they will arrive safely in due course and that you will be pleased with them. Our invoice is enclosed with the books.

The Leigh Hunt essays are not going to be so easy but we will see if we can find an attractive volume with them all in. We haven't the Latin Bible you describe but we have a Latin New Testament, also a Greek New Testament, ordinary modern editions in cloth binding. Would you like these?

Yours faithfully,

FPD
For MARKS & CO.

14 East 95th St.
New York City

November 3, 1949

Marks & Co.
84, Charing Cross Road
London, W.C. 2
England

Gentlemen:

The books arrived safely, the Stevenson is so fine it embarrasses my orange-crate bookshelves, I'm almost afraid to handle such soft vellum and heavy cream-colored pages. Being used to the dead-white paper and stiff cardboardy covers of American books, I never knew a book could be such a joy to the touch.

A Britisher whose girl lives upstairs translated the £1/17/6 for me and says I owe you $5.30 for the two books. I hope he got it right. I enclose a $5 bill and a single, please use the 70¢ toward the price of the New Testaments, both of which I want.

Will you please translate your prices hereafter? I don't add too well in plain American, I haven't a prayer of ever mastering bilingual arithmetic.

Yours,

Helene Hanff

I hope "madam" doesn't mean over there what it does here.

MARKS & CO., Booksellers
84, Charing Cross Road
London, W.C. 2

9th November, 1949

Miss Helene Hanff
14 East 95th Street
New York 28, New York
U.S.A.

Dear Miss Hanff,

Your six dollars arrived safely, but we should feel very much easier if you would send your remittances by postal money order in future, as this would be quite a bit safer for you than entrusting dollar bills to the mails.

We are very happy you liked the Stevenson so much. We have sent off the New Testaments, with an invoice listing the amount due in both pounds and dollars, and we hope you will be pleased with them.

Yours faithfully,

FPD
For MARKS & CO.

November 18, 1949

WHAT KIND OF A BLACK PROTESTANT BIBLE IS THIS?

Kindly inform the Church of England they have loused up the most beautiful prose ever written, whoever told them to tinker with the Vulgate Latin? They'll burn for it, you mark my words.

It's nothing to me, I'm Jewish myself. But I have a Catholic sister-in-law, a Methodist sister-in-law, a whole raft of Presbyterian cousins (through my Great-Uncle Abraham who converted) and an aunt who's a Christian Science healer, and I like to think none of them would countenance this Anglican Latin Bible if they knew it existed. (As it happens, they don't know Latin existed.)

Well, the hell with it. I've been using my Latin teacher's Vulgate, what I imagine I'll do is just not give it back till you find me one of my own.

I enclose $4 to cover the $3.88 due you, buy yourself a cup of coffee with the 12¢. There's no post office near here and I am not running all the way down to Rockefeller Plaza to stand in line for a $3.88 money order. If I wait till I get down there for something else, I won't have the $3.88 any more. I have implicit faith in the U.S. Airmail and His Majesty's Postal Service.

Have you got a copy of Landor's Imaginary Conversations? I think there are several volumes, the one I want is the one with the Greek conversations. If it contains a dialogue between Aesop and Rhodope, that'll be the volume I want.

Helene Hanff

MARKS & CO., Booksellers
84, Charing Cross Road
London, W.C. 2

26th November, 1949

Miss Helene Hanff
14 East 95th Street
New York 28, New York
U.S.A.

Dear Miss Hanff,

Your four dollars arrived safely and we have credited the 12 cents to your account.

We happen to have in stock Volume II of the Works & Life of Walter Savage Landor which contains the Greek dialogues including the one mentioned in your letter, as well as the Roman dialogues. It is an old edition published in 1876, not very handsome but well bound and a good clean copy, and we are sending it off to you today with invoice enclosed.

I am sorry we made the mistake with the Latin Bible and will try to find a Vulgate for you. Not forgetting Leigh Hunt.

Yours faithfully,

FPD
For MARKS & CO.

14 East 95th St.

New York City

December 8, 1949

Sir:

(It feels witless to keep writing "Gentlemen" when the same solitary soul is obviously taking care of everything for me.)

Savage Landor arrived safely and promptly fell open to a Roman dialogue where two cities had just been destroyed by war and everybody was being crucified and begging passing Roman soldiers to run them through and end the agony. It'll be a relief to turn to Aesop and Rhodope where all you have to worry about is a famine. I do love secondhand books that open to the page some previous owner read oftenest. The day Hazlitt came he opened to "I hate to read new books," and I hollered "Comrade!" to whoever owned it before me.

I enclose a dollar which Brian (British boy friend of Kay upstairs) says will cover the /8/ I owe you, you forgot to translate it.

Now then. Brian told me you are all rationed to 2 ounces of meat per family per week and one egg per person per month and I am simply appalled. He has a catalogue from a British firm here which flies food from Denmark to his mother, so I am sending a small Christmas present to Marks & Co. I hope there will be enough to go round, he says the Charing Cross Road bookshops are "all quite small."

I'm sending it c/o you, FPD, whoever you are.

Noel.

Helene Hanff

14 East 95th St.

December 9, 1949

FPD! CRISIS!

I sent that package off. The chief item in it was a 6-pound ham, I figured you could take it to a butcher and get it sliced up so everybody would have some to take home.

But I just noticed on your last invoice it says: "B. Marks. M. Cohen." Props.

ARE THEY KOSHER? I could rush a tongue over.

ADVISE PLEASE!

Helene Hanff

MARKS & CO., Booksellers
84, Charing Cross Road
London, W.C. 2

20th December, 1949

Miss Helene Hanff
14 East 95th Street
New York 28, New York
U.S.A.

Dear Miss Hanff,

Just a note to let you know that your gift parcel arrived safely today and the contents have been shared out between the staff. Mr. Marks and Mr. Cohen insisted that we divide it up among ourselves and not include "the bosses." I should just like to add that everything in the parcel was something that we either never see or can only be had through the black market. It was extremely kind and generous of you to think of us in this way and we are all extremely grateful.

We all wish to express our thanks and send our greetings and best wishes for 1950.

Yours faithfully,

Frank Doel
For MARKS & CO.

Frank Doel, what are you DOING over there, you are not doing ANYthing, you are just sitting AROUND.

Where is Leigh Hunt? Where is the Oxford Verse? Where is the Vulgate and dear goofy John Henry, I thought they'd be such nice uplifting reading for Lent and NOTHING do you send me.

you leave me sitting here writing long margin notes in library books that don't belong to me, some day they'll find out i did it and take my library card away.

I have made arrangements with the Easter bunny to bring you an Egg, he will get over there and find you have died of Inertia.

I require a book of love poems with spring coming on. No Keats or Shelley, send me poets who can make love without slobbering—Wyatt or Jonson or somebody, use your own judgment. Just a nice book preferably small enough to stick in a slacks pocket and take to Central Park.

Well, don't just sit there! Go find it! i swear i dont know how that shop keeps going.

MARKS & CO., Booksellers
84, Charing Cross Road
London, W.C. 2

7th April, 1950

Miss Helen Hanff
14 East 95th Street
New York 28, New York
U.S.A.

Dear Miss Hanff,

I have to thank you for the very welcome Easter parcel which arrived safely yesterday. We were all delighted to see the tins and the box of shell eggs, and the rest of the staff joins me in thanking you for your very kind and generous thought of us.

I am sorry we haven't been able to send you any of the books you want. About the book of love poems, now and then we do get such a volume as you describe. We have none in stock at the moment but shall look out for one for you.

Again, many thanks for the parcel.

Faithfully yours,

Frank Doel
For MARKS & CO.

84, Charing Cross Road
London, W.C. 2

7th April, 1950

Dear Miss Hanff,

Please don't let Frank know I'm writing this but every time I send you a bill I've been dying to slip in a little note and he might not think it quite proper of me. That sounds stuffy and he's not, he's quite nice really, very nice in fact, it's just that he does rather look on you as his private correspondent as all your letters and parcels are addressed to him. But I just thought I would write to you on my own.

We all love your letters and try to imagine what you must look like. I've decided you're young and very sophisticated and smart-looking. Old Mr. Martin thinks you must be quite studious-looking in spite of your wonderful sense of humor. Why don't you send us a snapshot? We should love to have it.

If you're curious about Frank, he's in his late thirties, quite nice-looking, married to a very sweet Irish girl, I believe she's his second wife.

Everyone was so grateful for the parcel. My little ones (girl 5, boy 4) were in Heaven—with the raisins and egg I was actually able to make them a cake!

I do hope you don't mind my writing. Please don't mention it when you write to Frank.

With best wishes,

Cecily Farr

P.S. I shall put my home address on the back of this in case you should ever want anything sent you from London.

C.F.

Dear Cecily—

And a <u>very</u> bad cess to Old Mr. Martin, tell him I'm so unstudious I never even went to college. I just happen to have peculiar taste in books, thanks to a Cambridge professor named Quiller-Couch, known as Q, whom I fell over in a library when I was 17. And I'm about as smart-looking as a Broadway panhandler. I live in moth-eaten sweaters and wool slacks, they don't give us any heat here in the daytime. It's a 5-story brownstone and all the other tenants go out to work at 9 A.M. and don't come home till 6—and why should the landlord heat the building for one small script-reader/writer working at home on the ground floor?

Poor Frank, I give him such a hard time, I'm always bawling him out for something. I'm only teasing, but I know he'll take me seriously. I keep trying to puncture that proper British reserve, if he gets ulcers I did it.

Please write and tell me about London, I live for the day when I step off the boat-train and feel its dirty sidewalks under my feet. I want to walk up Berkeley Square and down Wimpole Street and stand in St. Paul's where John Donne preached and sit on the step Elizabeth sat on when she refused to enter the Tower, and like that. A newspaper man I know, who was stationed in London during the war, says tourists go to England with preconceived notions, so they always find exactly what they go looking for. I told him I'd go looking for the England of English literature, and he said:

"Then it's there."

Regards—

Helene Hanff

MARKS & CO., Booksellers
84, Charing Cross Road
London, W.C. 2

20th September, 1950

Miss Helene Hanff
14 East 95th Street
New York 28, New York
U.S.A.

Dear Miss Hanff,

It is such a long time since we wrote to you I hope you do not think we have forgotten all about your wants.

Anyway, we now have in stock the Oxford Book of English Verse, printed on India paper, original blue cloth binding, 1905, inscription in ink on the flyleaf but a good secondhand copy, price $2.00. We thought we had better quote before sending, in case you have already purchased a copy.

Some time ago you asked us for Newman's Idea of a University. Would you be interested in a copy of the first edition? We have just purchased one, particulars as follows:

NEWMAN (JOHN HENRY, D.D.) Discourses on the Scope and Nature of University Education, Addressed to the Catholics of Dublin. First edition, 8vo. calf, Dublin, 1852. A few pages a little age-stained and spotted but a good copy in a sound binding.   Price—$6.00

In case you would like them, we will put both books on one side until you have time to reply.

With kind regards,
Yours faithfully,

Frank Doel
For MARKS & CO.

he has a first edition of Newman's University for six bucks, do i want it, he asks innocently.

Dear Frank:

Yes, I want it. I won't be fit to live with myself. I've never cared about first editions per se, but a first edition of THAT book—!

oh my.

i can just see it.

Send the <u>Oxford Verse</u>, too, please. Never wonder if I've found something somewhere else, I don't look anywhere else any more. Why should I run all the way down to 17th St. to buy dirty, badly made books when I can buy clean, beautiful ones from you without leaving the typewriter? From where I sit, London's a lot closer than 17th Street.

Enclosed please God please find $8. Did I tell you about Brian's lawsuit? He buys physics tomes from a technical book-shop in London, he's not sloppy and haphazard like me, he bought an expensive set and went down to Rockefeller Plaza and stood in line and got a money order and cabled it or whatever you do with it, he's a businessman, he does things right.

the money order got lost in transit.

Up His Majesty's Postal Service!

HH

am sending very small parcel to celebrate first edition, Overseas Associates finally sent me my own catalogue.

2nd October, 1950

Dear Helene,

I brought the enclosed snapshots to the shop with me weeks ago, but we've been frightfully busy so have had no chance to send them on to you. They were taken in Norfolk where Doug (my husband) is stationed with the RAF. None of them very flattering of me, but they are the best we have of the children and the one of Doug alone is very good.

My dear, I do hope you get your wish to come to England. Why not save your pennies and come next summer? Mummy and Daddy have a house in Middlesex and would be delighted to put you up.

Megan Wells (secretary to the bosses) and I are going on a week's holiday to Jersey (Channel Islands) in July. Why don't you come with us and then you could economize the rest of the month in Middlesex?

Ben Marks is trying to see what I'm writing so shall have to close.

Sincerely,

Cecily

14 East 95th St.

October 15, 1950

WELL!!!

All I have to say to YOU, Frank Doel, is we live in depraved, destructive and degenerate times when a bookshop—a BOOKSHOP—starts tearing up beautiful old books to use as wrapping paper. I said to John Henry when he stepped out of it:

"Would you believe a thing like that, Your Eminence?" and he said he wouldn't. You tore that book up in the middle of a major battle and I don't even know which war it was.

The Newman arrived almost a week ago and I'm just beginning to recover. I keep it on the table with me all day, every now and then I stop typing and reach over and touch it. Not because it's a first edition; I just never saw a book so beautiful. I feel vaguely guilty about owning it. All that gleaming leather and gold stamping and beautiful type belongs in the pine-panelled library of an English country home; it wants to be read by the fire in a gentleman's leather easy chair—not on a secondhand studio couch in a one-room hovel in a broken-down brownstone front.

I want the Q anthology. I'm not sure how much it was, I lost your last letter. I think it was about two bucks, I'll enclose two singles, if I owe you more let me know.

Why don't you wrap it in pages LCXII and LCXIII so I can at least find out who won the battle and what war it was?

HH

P.S. Have you got Sam Pepys' diary over there? I need him for long winter evenings.

MARKS & CO., Booksellers

84, Charing Cross Road

London, W.C. 2

1st November, 1950

Miss Helene Hanff
14 East 95th Street
New York 28, New York
U.S.A.

Dear Miss Hanff,

I am sorry for the delay in answering your letter but I have been away out of town for a week or so and am now busy trying to catch up on my correspondence.

First of all, please don't worry about us using old books such as Clarendon's Rebellion for wrapping. In this particular case they were just two odd volumes with the covers detached and nobody in their right senses would have given us a shilling for them.

The Quiller-Couch anthology, The Pilgrim's Way, has been sent to you by Book Post. The balance due was $1.85 so your $2 more than covered it. We haven't a copy of Pepys' Diary in stock at the moment but shall look out for one for you.

With best wishes,
Yours faithfully,

F. Doel
For MARKS & CO.

MARKS & CO., Booksellers
84, Charing Cross Road
London, W.C. 2

2nd February, 1951

Miss Helene Hanff
14 East 95th Street
New York 28, New York
U.S.A.

Dear Miss Hanff,

We are glad you liked the "Q" anthology. We have no copy of the Oxford Book of English Prose in stock at the moment but will try to find one for you.

About the Sir Roger de Coverley Papers, we happen to have in stock a volume of eighteenth century essays which includes a good selection of them as well as essays by Chesterfield and Goldsmith. It is edited by Austin Dobson and is quite a nice edition and as it is only $1.15 we have sent it off to you by Book Post. If you want a more complete collection of Addison & Steele let me know and I will try to find one.

There are six of us in the shop, not including Mr. Marks and Mr. Cohen.

Faithfully yours,

Frank Doel
For MARKS & CO.

Helene my dear—

There are many ways of doing it but Mummy and I think this is the simplest for you to try. Put a cup of flour, an egg, a half cup of milk and a good shake of salt into a large bowl and beat altogether until it is the consistency of thick cream. Put in the frig for several hours. (It's best if you make it in the morning.) When you put your roast in the oven, put in an extra pan to heat. Half an hour before your roast is done, pour a bit of the roast grease into the baking pan, just enough to cover the bottom will do. The pan must be very hot. Now pour the pudding in and the roast and pudding will be ready at the same time.

I don't know quite how to describe it to someone who has never seen it, but a good Yorkshire Pudding will puff up very high and brown and crisp and when you cut into it you will find that it is hollow inside.

The RAF is still keeping Doug in Norfolk and we are firmly hoarding your Christmas tins until he comes home, but my dear, what a celebration we shall have with them when he does! I do think you oughtn't to spend your money like that!

Must fly and post this if you're to have it for Brian's birthday dinner, do let me know if it's a success.

Love,

Cecily

February 25, 1951

Dear Cecily—

Yorkshire Pudding out of this world, we have nothing like it, I had to describe it to somebody as a high, curved, smooth, empty waffle.

Please don't worry about what the food parcels cost, I don't know whether Overseas Asso. is non-profit or duty-free or what, but they are monstrous cheap, that whole Christmas parcel cost less than my turkey. They do have a few rich parcels with things like standing rib-roasts and legs of lamb, but even those are so cheap compared with what they cost in the butcher shops that it kills me not to be able to send them. I have such a time with the catalogue, I spread it out on the rug and debate the relative merits of Parcel 105 (includes-one-dozen-eggs-and-a-tin-of-sweet-biscuits) and Parcel 217B (two-dozen-eggs-and-NO-sweet-biscuits), I hate the one-dozen egg parcels, what is two eggs for anybody to take home? But Brian says the powdered ones taste like glue. So it's a problem.

A producer who likes my plays (but not enough to produce them) just phoned. He's producing a TV series, do I want to write for television? "Two bills," he said carelessly, which it turned out means $200. And me a $40-a-week script-reader! I go down to see him tomorrow, keep your fingers crossed.

Best—

helene

4th April, 1951

Helene dear—

Your marvelous Easter parcels arrived safely and everyone is quite upset because Frank left the city on business for the firm the next morning and so hasn't written to thank you, and of course no one else quite dares to write to Frank's Miss Hanff.

My dear, the *meat!* I really don't think you should spend your money like that. It must have cost a packet! Bless you for your kind heart.

Here comes Ben Marks with work so must close.

Love,

Cecily

Earl's Terrace
Kensington High St.
London, W. 8

5th April, 1951

Dear Miss Hanff,

This is just to let you know that your Easter parcels to Marks & Co. arrived safely a few days ago but have not been acknowledged as Frank Doel is away from the office on business for the firm.

We were all quite dazzled to see the meat. And the eggs and tins were so very welcome. I did feel I must write and tell you how exceedingly grateful we all are for your kindness and generosity.

We all hope that you will be able to come to England one of these days. We should do our best to make your trip a happy one.

Sincerely,

Megan Wells

Tunbridge Road
Southend-On-Sea
Essex

5th April, 1951

Dear Miss Hanff:

For nearly two years I have been working as a cataloguer at Marks & Co. and would like to thank you very much for my share-out in the parcels which you've been sending.

I live with my great-aunt who is 75, and I think that if you had seen the look of delight on her face when I brought home the meat and the tin of tongue, you would have realized just how grateful we are. It's certainly good to know that someone so many miles away can be so kind and generous to people they haven't even seen, and I think that everyone in the firm feels the same.

If at any time you know of anything that you would like sent over from London, I will be most happy to see to it for you.

Sincerely,

Bill Humphries

MARKS & CO., Booksellers
84, Charing Cross Road
London, W.C. 2

9th April, 1951

Miss Helene Hanff
14 East 95th Street
New York 28, New York
U.S.A.

Dear Miss Hanff,

I expect you are getting a bit worried that we have not written to thank you for your parcels and are probably thinking that we are an ungrateful lot. The truth is that I have been chasing round the country in and out of various stately homes of England trying to buy a few books to fill up our sadly depleted stock. My wife was starting to call me the lodger who just went home for bed and breakfast, but of course when I arrived home with a nice piece of MEAT, to say nothing of dried eggs and ham, then she thought I was a fine fellow and all was forgiven. It is a long time since we saw so much meat all in one piece.

We should like to express our appreciation in some way or other, so we are sending by Book Post today a little book which I hope you will like. I remember you asked me for a volume of Elizabethan love poems some time ago—well, this is the nearest I can get to it.

Yours faithfully,

Frank Doel
For MARKS & CO.

To Helene Hanff, with best
wishes and grateful thanks for
many kindnesses, from all
at 84, Charing Cross Road, London.
April, 1951.

14 East 95th St.
New York City

April 16, 1951

To All at 84, Charing Cross Road:

Thank you for the beautiful book. I've never owned a book before with pages edged all round in gold. Would you believe it arrived on my birthday?

I wish you hadn't been so over-courteous about putting the inscription on a card instead of on the flyleaf. It's the bookseller coming out in you all, you were afraid you'd decrease its value. You would have increased it for the present owner. (And possibly for the future owner. I love inscriptions on flyleaves and notes in margins, I like the comradely sense of turning pages someone else turned, and reading passages some one long gone has called my attention to.)

And why didn't you sign your names? I expect Frank wouldn't let you, he probably doesn't want me writing love letters to anybody but him.

I send you greetings from America—faithless friend that she is, pouring millions into rebuilding Japan and Germany while letting England starve. Some day, God willing, I'll get over there and apologize personally for my country's sins (and by the time i come home my country will certainly have to apologize for mine).

Thank you again for the beautiful book, I shall try very hard not to get gin and ashes all over it, it's really much too fine for the likes of me.

Yours,

Helene Hanff

Dearheart—

It is the loveliest old shop straight out of Dickens, you would go absolutely out of your mind over it.

There are stalls outside and I stopped and leafed through a few things just to establish myself as a browser before wandering in. It's dim inside, you smell the shop before you see it, it's a lovely smell, I can't articulate it easily, but it combines must and dust and age, and walls of wood and floors of wood. Toward the back of the shop at the left there's a desk with a work-lamp on it, a man was sitting there, he was about fifty with a Hogarth nose, he looked up and said "Good afternoon?" in a North Country accent and I said I just wanted to browse and he said please do.

The shelves go on forever. They go up to the ceiling and they're very old and kind of grey, like old oak that has absorbed so much dust over the years they no longer are their true color. There's a print section, or rather a long print table, with Cruikshank and Rackham and Spy and all those old wonderful English caricaturists and illustrators that I'm not smart enough to know a lot about, and there are some lovely old, old illustrated magazines.

I stayed about half an hour hoping your Frank or one of the girls would turn up, but it was one-ish when I went in, I gather they were all out to lunch and I couldn't stay any longer.

As you see, the notices were not sensational but we're told they're good enough to assure us a few months' run, so I went apartment-hunting yesterday and found a nice little "bed-sitter" in Knightsbridge, I don't have the address here, I'll send it or you can call my mother.

We have no food problems, we eat in restaurants and hotels, the best places like Claridge's get all the roast beef and chops they want. The prices are astronomical but the exchange rate is so good we can afford it. Of course if I were the English I would loathe us, instead of which they are absolutely wonderful to us, we're invited to everybody's home and everybody's club.

The only thing we can't get is sugar or sweets in any form, for which I personally thank God, I intend to lose ten pounds over here.

Write me.

Love,

Maxine

Maxine, bless your golden heart, what a peachy description, you write better than I do.

I called your mother for your address, she said to tell you the sugar cubes and Nestle bars are on the way, I thought you were dieting?

I don't like to sound bitter, but I would like to know what YOU ever did that the good Lord lets YOU browse around my bookshop while I'm stuck on 95th St. writing the TV "Adventures of Ellery Queen." Did I tell you we're not allowed to use a lipstick-stained cigarette for a clue? We're sponsored by the Bayuk Cigar Co. and we're not allowed to mention the word "cigarette." We can have ashtrays on the set but they can't have any cigarette butts in them. They can't have cigar butts either, they're not pretty. All an ashtray can have in it is a wrapped, unsmoked Bayuk cigar.

And you hobnobbing with Gielgud at Claridge's.

Write me about London—the tube, the Inns of Court, Mayfair, the corner where the Globe Theatre stood, anything, I'm not fussy. Write me about Knightsbridge, it sounds green and gracious in Eric Coates' London Suite. Or London Again Suite.

xxxx

hh

14 East 95th St.

October 15, 1951

WHAT KIND OF A PEPYS' DIARY DO YOU CALL THIS?

this is not pepys' diary, this is some busybody editor's miserable collection of EXCERPTS from pepys' diary may he rot.

i could just spit.

where is jan. 12, 1668, where his wife chased him out of bed and round the bedroom with a red-hot poker?

where is sir w. pen's son that was giving everybody so much trouble with his Quaker notions? ONE mention does he get in this whole pseudo-book. and me from philadelphia.

i enclose two limp singles, i will make do with this thing till you find me a real Pepys. THEN i will rip up this ersatz book, page by page, AND WRAP THINGS IN IT.

HH

P.S. Fresh eggs or powdered for Xmas? I know the powdered last longer but "fresh farm eggs flown from Denmark" have got to taste better. you want to take a vote on it?

84, Charing Cross Road
London, W.C. 2

20th October, 1951

Miss Helene Hanff
14 East 95th Street
New York 28, New York
U.S.A.

Dear Miss Hanff,

First of all, let me apologize for the Pepys. I was honestly under the impression that it was the complete Braybrooke edition and I can understand how you must have felt when you found your favorite passages missing. I promise to look at the next reasonably priced copy that comes along, and if it contains the passage you mention in your letter I will send it along.

I am glad to say I have managed to dig out a few books for you from a private library that we have just bought. There is a Leigh Hunt which includes most of the essays you like, also a Vulgate New Testament which I hope will be O.K. I have also included a Dictionary to the Vulgate which you might find useful. There is also a volume of 20th century English essays, though it contains only one by Hilaire Belloc and nothing to do with bathrooms. Enclosed is our invoice for 17s 6d, or approximately $2.50, all that is due us on the books as you had a credit balance with us of nearly $2.00

About the eggs—I have talked to the rest of the inmates here and we all seem to think that the fresh ones would be nicer. As you say, they would not last so long but they would taste so much better.

We are all hoping for better times after the Election. If Churchill and Company get in, as I think and hope they will, it will cheer everyone up immensely.

With best wishes,
Yours sincerely,

Frank Doel
For MARKS & CO.

14 East 95th St.
New York City

November 2, 1951

Dear Speed—

You dizzy me, rushing Leigh Hunt and the Vulgate over here whizbang like that. You probably don't realize it, but it's hardly more than two years since I ordered them. You keep going at this rate you're gonna give yourself a heart attack.

that's mean. You go to so much trouble for me and i never even thank you, i just needle you, it's mean. I really am grateful for all the pains you take for me. I enclose three dollars, I'm sorry about the top one, I spilled coffee on it and it wouldn't sponge off but I think it's still good, you can still read it.

Do you carry hard-cover vocal scores, by any chance? Like Bach's St. Matthew Passion and Handel's Messiah? I could probably get them here at Schirmer's, but they're 50 cold blocks from where I live so I thought I'd ask you first.

Congratulations on Churchill & Co., hope he loosens up your rations a little.

Is your name Welsh?

HH

84, Charing Cross Road
London, W.C. 2

7th December, 1951

Miss Helene Hanff
14 East 95th Street
New York 28, New York

Dear Miss Hanff,

You will be glad to know that the two boxes of eggs and the tins of tongue have all arrived safely and once again we all wish to thank you most sincerely for your extreme generosity. Mr. Martin, one of the older members of our staff, has been on the sick list for some time and we therefore let him have the lion's share of the eggs, one whole boxful in fact, and of course he was delighted to get them. The tins of tongue look very inviting and will be a welcome addition to our larders, and in my case will be put on one side for a special occasion.

I enquired at all the local music shops but was unable to get the Messiah or Bach's St. Matthew Passion in stiff covers in clean, secondhand copies, and then I found they were available from the publisher in new editions. Their prices seemed a bit high, but I thought I had better get them and they have been sent by Book Post a few days ago, so should arrive any day now. Our invoice, total £1/10/ = ($4.20) is enclosed with the books.

We are sending you a little gift for Christmas. It is linen and we do hope you will not have to pay any duty on it. We will mark it "Christmas Gift" and keep our fingers crossed. Anyway, we hope you will like it and accept it with our sincere best wishes for Christmas and the coming year.

My name is certainly not of Welsh origin. As it is pronounced to rhyme with the French word "Noel," I think there may be a possibility that it originated in France.

Yours sincerely,

Frank Doel
For MARKS & CO.

Christmas Greetings
and
All Good Wishes for the
New Year
from

Geo. Martin   *Megan Wells*   *W. Humphries*
Cecily Farr   *Frank Doel*   *J. Pemberton*

MARKS & CO., Booksellers
84, Charing Cross Road
London, W.C. 2

15th January, 1952

Miss Helene Hanff
14 East 95th Street
New York 28, New York
U.S.A.

Dear Miss Hanff,

First of all, we were all so glad that you liked the cloth. It gave us a lot of pleasure to send it and it was one little way of thanking you for all your kind gifts over the last few years. You may be interested to know that it was embroidered, quite recently, by an old lady of over eighty who lives in the flat (apartment) next door to me. She lives all by herself and does quite a lot of needlework as a hobby. She does not often part with any of her work, but my wife managed to persuade her to sell this cloth, and I think she also made her a present of some of the dried egg you sent us which helped a lot.

If you must clean your Grolier Bible, we should advise ordinary soap and water. Put a teaspoonful of soda in a pint of warm water and use a soapy sponge. I think you will find this will remove the dirt and you can then polish it with a little lanolin.

J. Pemberton is a lady and the J. is for Janet.

With best wishes from all of us for the coming year.

Faithfully yours,

Frank Doel

Dear Miss Hanff:

For a long time I have wanted to write to you to thank you
for my family's share in the wonderful food parcels you've been
sending to Marks & Co. Now I have an excuse as Frank tells me
you want to know the name and address of the old lady who
embroidered your cloth. It was beautiful, wasn't it?

Her name is Mrs. Boulton and she lives next door at No.
36 Oakfield Court. She was thrilled to know that her cloth had
crossed the Atlantic and I know she would be delighted to hear
how much you admired it.

Thank you for wanting to send us more dried egg, but we
still have a bit left to see us through until spring. Some time
between April and September we usually manage all right for
eggs, as they go off ration for a time and then we do a bit of
trading with the tins, as once for a special occasion I traded a tin
of dried egg for a pair of nylons. Not quite legal but it does help
us to get by!

I will send you snaps of my happy family one of these
days. Our oldest girl was twelve last August, by name Sheila,
who by the way is my ready-made daughter, as Frank lost his
first wife during the war. Our youngest, Mary, was four last
week. Last May, Sheila announced at school that she was sending Mummy and Daddy an anniversary card and told the nuns
(it's a convent) that we had been married four years. It took a
bit of explaining as you can imagine.

I will close this with all good wishes for the New Year and especially a wish that we may see you in England one of these days.

Sincerely,

Nora Doel

36 Oakfield Court
Haslemere Road
Crouch End
London, N. 8

Jan. 29th, 1952

Dear Miss Hanff:

Thank you very much for your letter, I appreciate your kindness in telling me the cloth I worked has given you so much pleasure. I only wish I could do more. I expect Mrs. Doel has told you I am getting on in years so I am unable to do as much as I used to. It is always a joy to me when my work gets into the hands of someone who appreciates it.

I see Mrs. Doel most days, she often speaks of you. Perhaps I may see you if you come to England.

Again thanking you,

Yours very sincerely,

Mary Boulton

February 9, 1952

Now listen, Maxine—

I just talked to your mother, she says you don't think the show will run another month and she says you took two dozen pairs of nylons over there, so do me a favor. As soon as the closing notice goes up take four pairs of nylons around to the bookshop for me, give them to Frank Doel, tell him they're for the three girls and Nora (his wife).

Your mother says I am NOT to enclose any money for them, she got them last summer at a close-out sale at Saks, they were very cheap and she'll donate them to the shop, she's feeling pro-British.

Wait'll you see what the shop sent me for Christmas. It's an Irish linen tablecloth, the color of thick cream, hand-embroidered in an old-fashioned pattern of leaves and flowers, every flower worked in a different color and shaded from very pale to very deep, you never saw anything like it. My junk-shop drop-leaf table CERTainly never saw anything like it, i get this urge to shake out my flowing Victorian sleeve and lift a graceful arm to pour tea from an imaginary Georgian teapot, we're gonna play Stanislavski with it the minute you get home.

Ellery raised me to $250 a script, if it keeps up till June I may get to England and browse around my bookshop myself. If I have the nerve. I write them the most outrageous letters from a safe 3,000 miles away. i'll probably walk in there one day and walk right out again without telling them who i am.

I fail to see why you did not understand that groceryman, he did not call it "ground ground nuts," he called it "ground ground-nuts" which is the only really SENSible thing to call it. Peanuts grow in the GROUND and are therefore GROUND-nuts, and after you take them out of the ground you grind them up and you have <u>ground</u> ground-nuts, which is a much more accurate name than peanut butter, you just don't understand English.

XXX

h. hanff
girl etymologist

P.S. Your mother is setting out bravely this morning to look at an apartment for you on 8th Avenue in the 50's because you told her to look in the theatre district. Maxine you know perfectly well your mother is not equipped to look at ANYTHING on 8th Avenue.

SLOTH:

i could ROT over here before you'd send me anything to read. i oughta run straight down to brentano's which i would if anything i wanted was in print.

You may add Walton's Lives to the list of books you aren't sending me. It's against my principles to buy a book I haven't read, it's like buying a dress you haven't tried on, but you can't even get Walton's Lives in a library over here.

You can look at it. They have it down at the 42nd street branch. But not to take <u>home</u>! the lady said to me, shocked. eat it here. just sit right down in room 315 and read the whole book without a cup of coffee, a cigarette or air.

Doesn't matter, Q quoted enough of it so i know i'll like it. anything he liked i'll like except if it's fiction. i never can get interested in things that didn't happen to people who never lived.

what do you do with yourself all day, sit in the back of the store and read? why don't you try selling a book to somebody?

> *MISS Hanff to you.*
> (I'm helene only to my FRIENDS)

p.s. tell the girls and nora if all goes well they're getting nylons for Lent.

MARKS & CO., Booksellers
84, Charing Cross Road
London, W.C. 2

14th February, 1952

Miss Helene Hanff
14 East 95th Street
New York 28, New York
U.S.A.

Dear Helene,

I quite agree it is time we dropped the "Miss" when writing to you. I am not really so stand-offish as you may have been led to believe, but as copies of letters I have written to you go into the office files the formal address seemed more appropriate. But as this letter has nothing to do with books, there will be no copy.

We are quite at a loss to know how you managed the nylons which appeared this noon as if by magic. All I can tell you is that when I came back from lunch they were on my desk with a note reading: "From Helene Hanff." No one seems to know how or when they arrived. The girls are very thrilled and I believe they are planning to write to you themselves.

I am sorry to say that our friend Mr. George Martin who has been so ill for some time passed away in hospital last week. He was with the firm a great number of years, so with that loss and the King dying so suddenly as well, we are rather a mournful crowd at the moment.

I don't see how we can ever repay you for your many kind gifts. All I can say is, if you ever decide to make the trip to

England, there will be a bed for you at 37 Oakfield Court for as long as you care to stay.

With best wishes from us all,

Frank Doel

March 3, 1952

Oh my, i do bless you for that Walton's <u>Lives</u>. It's incredible that a book published in 1840 can be in such perfect condition more than a hundred years later. Such beautiful, mellow rough-cut pages they are, I do feel for poor William T. Gordon who wrote his name in it in 1841, what a crummy lot of descendants he must have—to sell it to you casually for nothing. Boy, I'd like to have run barefoot through THEIR library before they sold it.

fascinating book to read, did you know John Donne eloped with the boss's highborn daughter and landed in the Tower for it and starved and starved and THEN got religion. my word.

Now listen, I'm enclosing a $5 bill, that <u>Lives</u> makes me very dissatisfied with my <u>Angler</u> which I bought before I met you. It's one of those hard-faced American Classics-for-the-Masses editions, Izaak just hates it, he says he's not going around looking like THAT for the rest of my life, so use the extra $2.50 for a nice English <u>Angler,</u> please.

you better watch out. i'm coming over there in 53 if ellery is renewed. i'm gonna climb up that victorian book-ladder and disturb the dust on the top shelves and everybody's decorum. Or didn't I ever tell you I write arty murders for Ellery Queen on television? All my scripts have artistic backgrounds—ballet, concert hall, opera—and all the suspects and corpses are cultured. maybe I'll do one about the rare book business in your honor, you want to be the murderer or the corpse?

hh

36 Oakfield Court
Haslemere Road
Crouch End
London, N. 8

March 24th, 1952

Dear Miss Hanff:

I hardly know how to express my thanks and feelings for the lovely box of everything to eat which you have sent me which arrived today. I have never been sent a parcel before. I really don't think you should have done it. I can only say Thank you very much, I certainly will enjoy everything.

It was very kind of you to think of me in this way. I showed them all to Mrs. Doel, she thought they were lovely.

Again Thanking you very much, and best wishes,

Yours very sincerely,

Mary Boulton

MARKS & CO., Booksellers

84, Charing Cross Road
London, W.C. 2

17th April, 1952

Miss Helene Hanff
14 East 95th Street
New York 28, New York
U.S.A.

Dear Helene (you see I don't care about the files any more),

You will be pleased to know we have just purchased a private library which includes a very nice copy of Walton's Compleat Angler and hope to have it to send you next week, price approximately $2.25 and your credit balance with us is more than enough to cover it.

Your Ellery Queen scripts sound rather fun. I wish we could have the chance of seeing some of them on our TV over here—it wants livening up a bit (our TV I mean, not your script).

Nora and all here join me in sending our best wishes,

Yours faithfully,

Frank Doel

37 Oakfield Court
Haslemere Road
Crouch End
London, N. 8

Sunday, May 4th, 1952

Dear Helene,

Thanks for the parcel of dried egg received on Friday and I was very glad for same, I did mention something about eggs coming off the ration, well it just hasn't happened so the powder was a godsend for our weekend cakes, etc. Frank is taking some to the shop to send to Cecily, as he keeps forgetting to bring home her address. I expect you know she has left the shop and is waiting to join her husband in the East.

I am enclosing a few snaps, Frank says none of them do him justice, he is much better-looking; but we just let him dream.

Sheila was home for a month's break and we have been gadding about a bit to the seaside for day trips and sight-seeing and must now pull in our horns a bit, as the cost of transport here is terrific. It is our ambition to have a car but they are so expensive and a decent secondhand one is dearer than a new one. The new ones are being exported and there are so few for the home market some of my friends have been waiting 5 to 7 years for a new car.

Sheila is going to say a "jolly good prayer" for you so you may get your wish to come to England because the tin of bacon we had from you on Easter Monday was such a treat. So if "jolly good prayers" are answered you might have a windfall and be able to come and see us soon.

Well, so long for now and thanks once again.

Nora

14 East 95th St.
New York City

May 11, 1952

Dear Frank:

Meant to write you the day the <u>Angler</u> arrived, just to thank you, the woodcuts alone are worth ten times the price of the book. What a weird world we live in when so beautiful a thing can be owned for life—for the price of a ticket to a Broadway movie palace, or 1/50th the cost of having one tooth capped.

Well, if your books cost what they're worth I couldn't afford them!

You'll be fascinated to learn (from me that hates novels) that I finally got round to Jane Austen and went out of my mind over <u>Pride & Prejudice</u> which I can't bring myself to take back to the library till you find me a copy of my own.

Regards to Nora and the wage-slaves.

HH

Dear Helene:

Here I am again to thank you most gratefully for our share in the wonderful parcels you so kindly sent to Marks & Co. I wish I could send you something in return.

By the way, Helene, this week we have become the proud possessors of a car, not a new one, mind you, but it goes and that's what matters isn't it? Now maybe you will tell us you're paying us a call?

Mrs. Boulton put up two cousins of mine who came down from Scotland for a couple of weeks and they were very comfortable. She bedded them and I fed them. Now if by any chance you can manage the fare to England next year for the Coronation, Mrs. Boulton will see that you have a bed.

Well, I'll say so long for now and send you our best wishes and thanks once again for the meat and eggs.

Yours sincerely,

Nora

84, *Charing Cross Road*
London, W.C. 2

26th August, 1952

Miss Helene Hanff
14 East 95th Street
New York 28, New York
U.S.A.

Dear Helene,

I am writing once again to thank you on behalf of all here for your three very exciting parcels which arrived a few days ago. It is really too good of you to spend your hard-earned cash on us in this way and I can assure you that we do appreciate your kind thoughts of us.

We had about thirty volumes of Loeb Classics come in a few days ago but alas, no Horace, Sappho or Catullus.

I am taking a couple of weeks' holiday commencing September 1, but as I have just bought a car we are completely "broke" so will have to take things easy. Nora has a sister who lives by the sea so we are hoping she will take pity on us and invite us to stay with her. It is my first car so we are all very thrilled with it—even though it is an old 1939 model. So long as it gets us to places without breaking down too often we shall be quite happy.

With all good wishes,

Frank Doel

Frankie, guess who came while you were away on vacation?
SAM PEPYS! Please thank whoever mailed him for me, he
came a week ago, stepped out of four pages of some tabloid,
three honest navy-blue volumes of him; I read the tabloid over
lunch and started Sam after dinner.

He says to tell you he's overJOYED to be here, he was
previously owned by a slob who never even bothered to cut the
pages. I'm wrecking them, it's the thinnest India paper I ever
saw. We call it "onion skin" over here and it's a good name for
it. But heavier paper would have taken up six or seven volumes
so I'm grateful for the India. I only have three bookshelves and
very few books left to throw out.

I houseclean my books every spring and throw out those
I'm never going to read again like I throw out clothes I'm never
going to wear again. It shocks everybody. My friends are peculiar about books. They read all the best sellers, they get through
them as fast as possible, I think they skip a lot. And they
NEVER read anything a second time so they don't remember a
word of it a year later. But they are profoundly shocked to see
me drop a book in the wastebasket or give it away. The way
they look at it, you buy a book, you read it, you put it on the
shelf, you never open it again for the rest of your life but YOU
DON'T THROW IT OUT! NOT IF IT HAS A HARD
COVER ON IT! Why not? I personally can't think of anything
less sacrosanct than a bad book or even a mediocre book.

Trust you and Nora had a fine holiday. Mine was spent in
Central Park, I had a month's vacation from joey, my dear little
dentist, he went on his honeymoon. i financed the honeymoon.

Did I tell you he told me last spring I had to have all my teeth capped or all my teeth out? I decided to have them capped as I have got used to having teeth. But the cost is simply astronomical. So Elizabeth will have to ascend the throne without me, teeth are all I'm going to see crowned for the next couple of years.

i do NOT intend to stop buying books, however, you have to have SOMEthing. Will you see if you can find me Shaw's dramatic criticism please? and also his music criticism? I think there are several volumes, just send whatever you can find, now listen, Frankie, it's going to be a long cold winter and I baby-sit in the evenings AND I NEED READING MATTER, NOW DON'T START SITTING AROUND, GO FIND ME SOME BOOKS.

hh

To "her friends at 84, Charing Cross Road":

The Book-Lovers' Anthology stepped out of its wrappings, all gold-embossed leather and gold-tipped pages, easily the most beautiful book I own including the Newman first edition. It looks too new and pristine ever to have been read by anyone else, but it has been: it keeps falling open at the most delightful places as the ghost of its former owner points me to things I've never read before. Like Tristram Shandy's description of his father's remarkable library which "contained every book and treatise which had ever been wrote upon the subject of great noses." (Frank! Go find me Tristram Shandy!)

I do think it's a very uneven exchange of Christmas presents. You'll eat yours up in a week and have nothing left to show for it by New Year's Day. I'll have mine till the day I die —and die happy in the knowledge that I'm leaving it behind for someone else to love. I shall sprinkle pale pencil marks through it pointing out the best passages to some booklover yet unborn.

Thank you all. Happy New Year.

Helene

37 Oakfield Court
Haslemere Road
Crouch End
London, N. 8

17–12–52

Dear Helene:

So sorry I have been so long in dropping you a line. I hope you haven't taken it too badly about Adlai. Maybe he will have better luck next time.

Mrs. Boulton says she will gladly put you up next summer if she is still alive, she says, but I don't know of anyone of her age who is more so, I feel sure she will live to be a hundred. Anyway, we can always fix you up somewhere.

Thanks for the good things you sent us for Christmas, you are much too kind, Helene!—and if those bodies at Marks & Co. don't give you a banquet when you come over next year, well, they deserve to be shot.

I hope you have a lovely Christmas. Cheerio for now and all our best wishes and thanks.

God bless!

Nora

14 East 95th St.

May 3, 1953

Frankie, you'll DIE when I tell you—

First, enclosed find $3, P-and-P arrived looking exactly as Jane ought to look, soft leather, slim and impeccable.

Now then. Ellery went off the air and I was shuffling around piling up dentist bills and feeling pale when I was invited to write an outline for a TV show which dramatizes incidents from the lives of famous people. So I rushed home and did an outline of an incident from-the-life-of-a-famous-person and sent it in and they bought it and I wrote the script and they liked it and they're gonna give me more work in the fall.

And whaddaya think I dramatized? JOHN DONNE ELOPING WITH THE BOSS'S DAUGHTER out of Walton's Lives. Nobody who watches television has the slightest idea who John Donne was, but thanks to Hemingway everybody knows No Man Is An Island, all I had to do was work that in and it was sold.

So that's how John Donne made the "Hallmark Hall of Fame" and paid for all the books you ever sent me and five teeth.

I plan to crawl out of bed before dawn on Coronation Day to attend the ceremony by radio. Will be thinking of you all.

cheers

hh

MARKS & CO., Booksellers
84, Charing Cross Road
London, W.C. 2

11th June, 1953

Miss Helene Hanff
14 East 95th Street
New York 28, New York
U.S.A.

Dear Helene,

Just a note to let you know that your parcel arrived safely on June 1, just in time for our Coronation Day celebrations. We had a number of friends at home to watch TV on the day, and so the ham was most welcome to provide them with something to eat. It was delicious, and we all drank your health as well as the Queen's.

It was most kind of you to spend your hard-earned money on us like this, and the rest of the staff join me in saying thanks a lot.

With very best wishes,
Yours sincerely,

Frank Doel

Boldmere Road
Eastcote
Pinner
Middlesex

23–9–53

Helene dear,

Am dashing this off to say you must send <u>nothing at all</u> to the shop for Christmas, everything is now off rations and even nylons are available in all the better shops. Please save your money as the most important thing after your dentist is your trip to England. Only don't come in '54 as I shall be out of the country, come in '55 when we shall be back and you can stay with us.

Doug writes that our "call" may come at any moment as we are next in line for married quarters. The children and I are hoping to join him before Christmas. He is well and happy on Bahrein Island in the middle of the Persian Gulf (if you've got an atlas) but will return to the RAF base at Habbaniya in Iraq when our quarters are available and we will join him there, all being well.

Write again soon. Even if I do "pop off" Mother will forward your letter.

Love and best wishes—

Cecily

DO YOU MEAN TO SIT THERE AND TELL ME YOU'VE
BEEN PUBLISHING THESE MAMMOTH CATALOGUES
ALL THESE YEARS AND THIS IS THE FIRST TIME
YOU EVER BOTHERED TO SEND ME ONE? THOU
VARLET?

Don't remember which restoration playwright called everybody a Varlet, i always wanted to use it in a sentence.

As it happens, the only thing which MIGHT interest me is
the Catullus, it's not the Loeb Classics but it sounds like it'll do.
If you still have it, mail it and I'll send you the -/6s/2d as soon
as you translate it, Kay and Brian moved to the suburbs and left
me without a translator.

I shall be obliged if you will send Nora and the girls to
church every Sunday for the next month to pray for the con-
tinued health and strength of the messrs. gilliam, reese, snider,
campanella, robinson, hodges, furillo, podres, newcombe and
labine, collectively known as The Brooklyn Dodgers. If they lose
this World Series I shall Do Myself In and then where will you
be?

Have you got De Tocqueville's Journey to America? Somebody borrowed mine and never gave it back. Why is it that
people who wouldn't dream of stealing anything else think it's
perfectly all right to steal books?

Regards to Megan if she's still there. And what's become
of Cecily, is she back from Iraq?

h.h.

84, Charing Cross Road
London, W.C. 2

13th December, 1955

Miss Helene Hanff
14 East 95th Street
New York 28, N.Y.
U.S.A.

Dear Helene,

I feel very guilty about not writing to you before this, but you can put it down to a dose of 'flu which kept me away from the shop for a couple of weeks and a sudden rush of work since I came back.

About the Catullus in our catalogue. This was already sold before we received your letter but I have sent you an edition which contains the Latin text with a verse translation by Sir Richard Burton and also a prose translation by Leonard Smithers, printed in large type, and all for $3.78. The binding is not very handsome but it's a good clean copy. We have no edition of De Tocqueville but will keep looking for one for you.

Megan is still here but planning to go to South Africa to live, we are all trying to talk her out of it. We have heard nothing from Cecily Farr since she went out to the East to join her husband, though they were only to be gone a year.

I shall be only too pleased to root for the Brooklyn Dodgers if you will reciprocate with a few cheers for THE SPURS (the Tottenham Hotspurs Football Club to the uninitiated), who are at present languishing next to the bottom of the League. However, the season does not finish until next April so they have plenty of time to get themselves out of the mess.

Nora and all here join me in sending our best wishes for Christmas and the New Year.

Sincerely,

Frank Doel

14 e. 95th st.

nyc

jan. 4, 1956

i write you from under the bed where that catullus drove me.

i mean it PASSETH understanding.

Up till now, the only Richard Burton I ever heard of is a handsome young actor I've seen in a couple of British movies and I wish I'd kept it that way. This one got knighted for turning Catullus—caTULLus—into Victorian hearts-and-flowers.

and poor little mr. smithers must have been afraid his mother was going to read it, he like to KILL himself cleaning it all up.

all right, let's just you go find me a nice plain Latin Catullus, I bought myself a Cassell's dictionary, I'll work out the hard passages by myself.

WILL YOU TELL MEGAN WELLS SHE IS OUT OF HER COTTONPICKING MIND? if she's that bored with civilization why doesn't she just move to a siberian salt mine?

certainly, certainly, glad to root for anything with Hotspur in it.

Have been socking money in the savings bank for next summer, if TV keeps feeding me till then I'm finally coming over, I want to see the shop and St. Paul's and Parliament and the Tower and Covent Garden and the Old Vic and Old Mrs. Boulton.

i enclose a sawbuck for that thing. that catullus. bound in white Limp—mit-white-silk-bookmark-yet, frankie, where do you FIND these things?!

hh

MARKS & CO., Booksellers

84, Charing Cross Road

London, W.C. 2

16th March, 1956

Miss Helene Hanff
14 East 95th Street
New York 28, N.Y.
U.S.A.

Dear Helene,

I am sorry to have been so long in writing, but until today we have had nothing to send you and I thought it best to wait a decent interval after the Catullus incident before writing.

We have finally managed to find a very nice edition of Tristram Shandy with the Robb illustrations, price approximately $2.75. We have also acquired a copy of Plato's Four Socratic Dialogues, translated by Benjamin Jowett, Oxford, 1903. Would you like this for $1.00? You have a $1.22 credit with us so the balance due on the two books would be $2.53.

We are waiting to hear whether you are finally coming to England this summer. Both the girls are away at school so you will have your choice of beds at 37 Oakfield Court. I am sorry to say that Mrs. Boulton has been taken to a home, it was rather a sad day but at least she will be looked after there.

Sincerely,

Frank Doel

14 East 95th St.
New York City

June 1, 1956

Dear Frank:

Brian introduced me to Kenneth Grahame's Wind in the Willows and I have to have this—with the Shepard illustrations please—but DON'T MAIL IT, JUST HOLD IT FOR ME TILL SEPTEMBER and then mail it to the new address.

The sky fell on us in this cozy brownstone, we got eviction notices last month, they're renovating the building. I decided the time had come to get me a real apartment with real furniture, and in my right mind and shaking all over I went around to the construction site of a new building going up over on 2nd Avenue and signed a lease on a 2½ ("bed-sitter") apartment that isn't even there yet. I am now racing around buying furniture and bookshelves and wall-to-wall carpet with all my England money, but all my life I've been stuck in dilapidated furnished rooms and cockroachy kitchens and I want to live like a lady even if it means putting off England till it's paid for.

Meanwhile the landlord thinks we're not moving out fast enough and is encouraging us by firing the super, leaving nobody to give us hot water or take the garbage out, and also by ripping out the mailboxes, the hall light fixtures and (as of this week) the wall between my kitchen and bathroom. all this and the dodgers disintegrating before my very eyes, nobody-knows-the-trouble-i-see.

Oh, the new address:

AFTER SEPTEMBER 1:
305 E. 72nd St., New York, N.Y. 21

84, Charing Cross Road
London, W.C. 2

3rd May, 1957

Miss Helene Hanff
305 East 72nd Street
New York 21, N.Y.
U.S.A.

Dear Helene,

Prepare yourself for a shock. ALL THREE of the books you requested in your last letter are on the way to you and should arrive in a week or so. Don't ask how we managed it—it's just a part of the Marks service. Our bill is enclosed herewith showing balance due of $5.00

Two of your friends dropped in to see us a few days ago and now I have forgotten their names—a young married couple and very charming. Unfortunately they only had time to stop and smoke a cigarette as they were off again on their travels next morning.

We seem to have had more American visitors than ever this year, including hundreds of lawyers who march around with a large card pinned to their clothes stating their home town and name. They all seem to be enjoying their trip so you will have to manage it next year.

With best wishes from us all,

Frank

You might have warned us! We walked into your book-store and said we were friends of yours and were nearly mobbed. Your Frank wanted to take us home for the weekend. Mr. Marks came out from the back of the store just to shake hands with friends-of-Miss-Hanff, everybody in the place wanted to wine and dine us, we barely got out alive.

Thought you'd like to see the house where your Sweet-William was born.

On to Paris, then Copenhagen, home on the 23rd.

Love,

Ginny and Ed

January 10, 1958

Hey, Frankie—

Tell Nora to bring her address book up to date, your Christmas card just got here, she sent it to 14 e. 95th st.

Don't know whether I ever told you how dearly I love that Tristram Shandy, the Robb illustrations are enchanting, Uncle Toby would have been pleased. Now then. In the back, there's a list of other Macdonald Illustrated Classics which includes the Essays of Elia. I'd love to have this in the Macdonald edition— or any nice edition. If it's Reasonable, of course. Nothing's cheap any more, it's "reasonable." Or "sensibly priced." There's a building going up across the street, the sign over it says:

> "One and Two Bedroom Apartments
> At Rents That Make Sense."

Rents do NOT make sense. And prices do not sit around being reasonable about anything, no matter what it says in the ad— which isn't an ad any more, it's A Commercial.

i go through life watching the english language being raped before me face. like miniver cheevy, i was born too late.

and like miniver cheevy i cough and call it fate and go on drinking.

hh

p.s. whatever became of plato's minor dialogues?

MARKS & CO., Booksellers

84, Charing Cross Road

London, W.C. 2

11th March, 1958

Miss Helene Hanff
305 East 72nd Street
New York 21, New York
U.S.A.

Dear Helene,

I must apologize for having taken so long to answer your last letter but we have had rather a hectic time. Nora has been in hospital for the past several months and I have had my hands full at home. She is almost fully recovered and will be coming home in a week or so. It has been a trying time for us but thanks to our National Health Service it hasn't cost us a penny.

About the Macdonald Classics, we do get a few from time to time but have none at the moment. We had several copies of Lamb's Essays of Elia earlier on but they were snapped up during the holiday rush. I am off on a buying trip next week and will look out for one for you. Not forgetting the Plato.

We all hope you had a good holiday season and the girls apologize for sending your Christmas card to the old address.

Faithfully yours,

Frank

37 Oakfield Court
Haslemere Road
Crouch End
London, N. 8

May 7th, 1958

Dear Helene,

I have to thank you for your two letters, thanks for the offer, Helene, but there is really nothing we need. I wish we had our own bookshop, then we would be able to repay your kindness by sending you a few books.

I am enclosing a few recent snaps of my happy family, I wish they were better but we seem to have given all the best ones to relatives. You will probably notice how very much alike Sheila and Mary are. It is rather noticeable. Frank says that Mary, as she has been growing up, is exactly like Sheila was at the same age. Sheila's mother was Welsh and I hail from the Emerald Isle so they both must resemble Frank but they are better-looking than he is, though of course he won't admit this!

If you knew how much I hate writing you would feel sorry for me. Frank says for one who talks so much I put up a very bad show on paper.

Again thanks for the letters and good wishes.

God bless!

Nora

MARKS & CO., Booksellers
84, Charing Cross Road
London, W.C. 2

18th March, 1959

Miss Helene Hanff
305 East 72nd Street
New York 21, New York
U.S.A.

Dear Helene,

I don't know how to break the bad news, but two days after offering you the Shorter Oxford Dictionary for your friend, a man came in and bought it when my back was turned. I have delayed replying to your letter in the hope that another one would come along, but no luck yet. I am terribly sorry to disappoint your friend but you can blame it all on me as I really ought to have reserved it.

We are sending off by Book Post today the Johnson on Shakespeare, which we happened to have in stock in the Oxford Press edition with introduction by Walter Raleigh. It is only $1.05 and your balance with us was more than enough to cover it.

We are all sorry to hear that your television shows have moved to Hollywood and that one more summer will bring us every American tourist but the one we want to see. I can quite understand your refusal to leave New York for Southern California. We have our fingers crossed for you and hope that some sort of work will turn up soon.

Sincerely,

Frank

August 15, 1959

sir:

i write to say i have got work.

i won it. i won a $5,000 Grant-in-Aid off CBS, it's supposed to support me for a year while I write American History dramatizations. I am starting with a script about New York under seven years of British Occupation and i MARVEL at how i rise above it to address you in friendly and forgiving fashion, your behavior over here from 1776 to 1783 was simply FILTHY.

Is there such a thing as a modern-English version of the Canterbury Tales? I have these guilts about never having read Chaucer but I was talked out of learning Early Anglo-Saxon/-Middle English by a friend who had to take it for her Ph.D. They told her to write an essay in Early Anglo-Saxon on any-subject-of-her-own-choosing. "Which is all very well," she said bitterly, "but the only essay subject you can find enough Early Anglo-Saxon words for is 'How to Slaughter a Thousand Men in a Mead Hall.' "

She also filled me in on Beowulf and his illegitimate son Sidwith—or is it Widsith? she says it's not worth reading so that killed my interest in the entire subject, just send me a modern Chaucer.

love to nora.

hh

MARKS & CO., Booksellers

84, Charing Cross Road
London, W.C. 2

2nd September, 1959

Miss Helene Hanff
305 East 72nd Street
New York 21, New York
U.S.A.

Dear Helene,

    We were all delighted to hear that you've won a Grant-in-Aid and are working again. We are prepared to be broad-minded about your choice of subject matter, but I must tell you that one of the young inmates here confessed that until he read your letter he never knew that England had ever owned "the States."

    With regard to Chaucer, the best scholars seem to have fought shy of putting him into modern English, but there was an edition put out by Longmans in 1934, the Canterbury Tales only, a modernized version by Hill, which I believe is quite good. It is (of course!) out of print and I am trying to find a nice clean secondhand copy.

Sincerely,

Frank

i don't know, frankie—

Somebody gave me this book for Christmas. It's a Giant Modern Library book. Did you ever see one of those? It's less attractively bound than the Proceedings of the New York State Assembly and it weighs more. It was given to me by a gent who knows I'm fond of John Donne. The title of this book is:

The Complete Poetry
&
Selected Prose
of
JOHN DONNE
&
The Complete Poetry
of
WILLIAM BLAKE?

The question mark is mine. Will you please tell me what those two boys have in common?—except they were both English and they both Wrote? I tried reading the Introduction figuring that might explain it. The Introduction is in four parts. Parts I and II include a Professor's life of Donne mit-illustrations-from-the-author's-works-also-criticism. Part III begins—and God knows I quote—:

> When, as a little boy, William Blake saw the prophet Ezekiel under a tree amid a summer field, he was soundly trounced by his mother.

I'm with his mother. I mean, the back of the Lord God or the face of the Virgin Mary, all right—but why the hell would anybody want to see the prophet Ezekiel?

I don't like Blake anyway, he swoons too much, it's Donne I'm writing about, I am being driven clear up the wall, Frankie, you have GOT to help me.

Here I was, curled up in my armchair so at peace with the world, with something old and serene on the radio—Corelli or somebody—and this thing on the table. This Giant Modern Library thing. So I thought:

"I will read the three standard passages from Sermon XV aloud," you have to read Donne aloud, it's like a Bach fugue.

Would you like to know what I went through in an innocent attempt to read three contiguous uncut passages from Sermon XV aloud?

You start with the Giant Modern Library version, you locate Sermon XV and there they are: Excerpts I, II and III,—only when you get to the end of Excerpt I you discover they have deleted Jezebel off it. So you get down Donne's Sermons, Selected Passages (Logan Pearsall Smith) where you spend twenty minutes locating Sermon XV, Excerpt I, because by Logan Pearsall Smith it isn't Sermon XV, Excerpt I, it's Passage 126. All Must Die. Now that you've found it, you find he also deleted Jezebel so you get down the Complete Poetry & Selected Prose (Nonesuch Press) but they didn't happen to Select Jezebel either, so you get down the Oxford Book of English Prose where you spend another twenty minutes locating it because in the Oxford English Prose it isn't Sermon XV, Excerpt I nor yet 126. All Must Die, it's Passage 113. Death the Leveller. Jezebel is there, and you read it aloud but when you get to the end you find it doesn't have either Excerpt II or III so you have to switch to one of the other three books provided you had the wit to leave all three open at the right pages which I didn't.

So break it to me gently: how hard is it going to be to find me John Donne's Complete Sermons and how much is it going to cost?

i am going to bed. i will have hideous nightmares involving

huge monsters in academic robes carrying long bloody butcher knives labelled Excerpt, Selection, Passage and Abridged.

yrs,

h. hffffffffffffff

MARKS & CO., Booksellers

84, Charing Cross Road
London, W.C. 2

5th March, 1960

Miss Helene Hanff
305 East 72nd Street
New York 21, New York
U.S.A.

Dear Helene,

I have delayed answering your last two letters until I had some good news to report. I have managed to obtain a copy of the Bernard Shaw–Ellen Terry correspondence. It is not a very attractive edition but it is a good clean copy and I thought I had better send it as this is quite a popular book and it might be quite some time before another copy comes along. The price is approximately $2.65 and you have a credit with us of 50 cents.

I am afraid the complete Donne Sermons can be had only by buying Donne's Complete Works. This runs to more than 40 volumes and would be very expensive if in good condition.

We hope you had a good Christmas and New Year in spite of the Giant Modern Library.

Nora joins me in sending best wishes.

Sincerely,

Frank

May 8, 1960

M. De Tocqueville's compliments and he begs to announce his safe arrival in America. He sits around looking smug because everything he said was true, especially about lawyers running the country. i belong to a Democratic club, there were fourteen men over there the other night, eleven of them lawyers. came home and read a couple of newspaper stories about the presidential hopefuls—stevenson, humphrey, kennedy, stassen, nixon—all lawyers but humphrey.

I enclose three bucks, it's a beautiful book and you can't even call it secondhand, the pages weren't cut. Did I tell you I finally found the perfect page-cutter? It's a pearl-handled fruit knife. My mother left me a dozen of them, I keep one in the pencil cup on my desk. Maybe I go with the wrong kind of people but i'm just not likely to have twelve guests all sitting around simultaneously eating fruit.

cheers

hh

February 2, 1961

Frank?

You still there?

i swore i wouldn't write till i got work.

Sold a story to Harper's Magazine, slaved over it for three weeks and they paid me $200 for it. Now they've got me writing the story of my life in a book. they're "advancing" me $1,500 to write it and they figure it shouldn't take me more than six months. I don't mind for myself but the landlord worries.

so I can't buy any books but back in October somebody introduced me to Louis the Duke de Saint-Simon in a miserable abridgement, and I tore around to the Society Library where they let you roam the stacks and lug everything home, and got the real thing. Have been wallowing in Louis ever since. The edition I'm reading is in six volumes and halfway through Vol. VI last night I realized I could not supPORT the notion that when I take it back I will have NO louis in the house.

The translation I'm reading is by Francis Arkwright and it's delightful but I'll settle for any edition you can find that you trust. DO NOT MAIL IT! just buy it and let me know what it costs and keep it there and I'll buy it from you one volume at a time.

Hope Nora and the girls are fine. And you. And anybody else who knows me.

Helene

MARKS & CO., Booksellers

84, Charing Cross Road
London, W.C. 2

15th February, 1961

Miss Helene Hanff
305 East 72nd Street
New York 21, N.Y.

Dear Helene,

You will be pleased to know that we have a copy of the
Memoirs of the Duke de Saint-Simon in stock in the Arkwright
translation, six volumes nicely bound and in very good condition. We are sending them off to you today and they should
arrive within a week or two. The amount due on them is
approximately $18.75 but please don't worry about paying it all
at once. Your credit will always be good at Marks & Co.

It was very good to hear from you again. We are all well,
and still hoping to see you in England one of these days.

Love from us all,

Frank

March 10, 1961

Dear Frankie—

Enclosed-please-God-please-find a $10 bill, it better get there, not many of those float in here these days but louis wanted me to get him paid off, he got so tired of the deadbeats at court he didn't want to move in with one 270 years later.

Thought of you last night, my editor from Harper's was here for dinner, we were going over this story-of-my-life and we came to the story of how I dramatized Landor's "Aesop and Rhodope" for the "Hallmark Hall of Fame." Did I ever tell you that one? Sarah Churchill starred as Landor's dewy-eyed Rhodope. The show was aired on a Sunday afternoon. Two hours before it went on the air, I opened the New York Times Sunday book review section and there on page 3 was a review of a book called A House Is Not a Home by Polly Adler, all about whorehouses, and under the title was the photo of a sculptured head of a Greek girl with a caption reading: "Rhodope, the most famous prostitute in Greece." Landor had neglected to mention this. Any scholar would have known Landor's Rhodope was the Rhodopis who took Sappho's brother for every dime he had but I'm not a scholar, I memorized Greek endings one stoic winter but they didn't stay with me.

So we were going over this anecdote and Gene (my editor) said "Who is Landor?" and I plunged into an enthusiastic explanation—and Gene shook her head and cut in impatiently:

"You and your Olde English books!"

You see how it is, frankie, you're the only soul alive who understands me.

xx

hh

p.s. Gene's Chinese.

MARKS & CO., Booksellers
84, Charing Cross Road
London, W.C. 2

14th October, 1963

Miss Helene Hanff
305 East 72nd Street
New York 21, N.Y.
U.S.A.

Dear Helene,

You will no doubt be surprised to learn that the two volumes of Virginia Woolf's Common Reader are on their way to you. If you want anything else I can probably get it for you with the same efficiency and swiftness.

We are all well and jogging along as usual. My eldest daughter Sheila (24) suddenly decided she wanted to be a teacher so threw up her secretarial job two years ago to go to college. She has another year to go so it looks as though it will be a long time before our children will be able to keep us in luxury.

Love from all here,

Frank

MARKS & CO., Booksellers
84, Charing Cross Road
London, W.C. 2

9th November, 1963

Miss Helene Hanff
305 East 72nd Street
New York 21, New York
U.S.A.

Dear Helene,

Some time ago you asked me for a modern version of Chaucer's <u>Canterbury Tales</u>. I came across a little volume the other day which I thought you would like. It is not complete by any means, but as it is quite a cheap book and seems to be a fairly scholarly job, I am sending it along by Book Post today, price $1.35. If this whets your appetite for Chaucer and you would like something more complete later on, let me know and I will see what I can find.

Sincerely,

Frank

All right, that's enough Chaucer-made-easy, it has the schoolroom smell of Lamb's Tales from Shakespeare.

I'm glad i read it. i liked reading about the nun who ate so dainty with her fingers she never dripped any grease on herself. I've never been able to make that claim and I use a fork. Wasn't anything else that intrigued me much, it's just stories, I don't like stories. Now if Geoffrey had kept a diary and told me what it was like to be a little clerk in the palace of richard III— THAT I'd learn Olde English for. I just threw out a book somebody gave me, it was some slob's version of what it was like to live in the time of Oliver Cromwell—only the slob didn't LIVE in the time of Oliver Cromwell so how the hell does he know what it was like? Anybody wants to know what it was like to live in the time of Oliver Cromwell can flop on the sofa with Milton on his pro side and Walton on his con, and they'll not only tell him what it was like, they'll take him there.

"The reader will not credit that such things could be," Walton says somewhere or other, "but I was there and I saw it."

that's for me, I'm a great lover of i-was-there books.

i enclose two bucks for the chaucer, that leaves me a credit with you of 65¢ which is a larger credit than i have anywhere else.

xx

h

86

March 30, 1964

Dear Frank—

I take time out from a children's history book (my fourth, would you believe?) to ask if you can help a friend. He has an incomplete set of Shaw in what he insists is just called the Standard Edition. It's bound in rust-colored cloth, he says, if that helps. I enclose a list of what he has, he wants all the others in the set but if you have more than a few, don't send them all at once. He'll buy them piecemeal, like me he's a pauper. Send them to him direct, to the address on the list. That's 32nd Avenue in case you can't read it.

Do you ever hear anything of Cecily or Megan?

best

helene

MARKS & CO., Booksellers
84, Charing Cross Road
London, W.C. 2

14th April, 1964

Miss Helene Hanff
305 East 72nd Street
New York 21, New York
U.S.A.

Dear Helene,

About the Shaw for your friend, the Standard Edition is still available from the publishers, it is bound in the rust-coloured cloth as he describes and I think there are about 30 volumes in the complete set. Used copies seldom come along but if he would like us to send him new copies we shall be glad to do so and could send him three or four volumes a month.

We have not heard from Cecily Farr in some years now. Megan Wells had enough of South Africa in a very short time and did stop in to give us a chance to say I-told-you-so, before going out to try her luck in Australia. We had a Christmas card from her a few years ago but nothing recently.

Nora and the girls join me in sending love,

Frank

MARKS & CO., Booksellers
84, Charing Cross Road
London, W.C. 2

4th October, 1965

Miss Helene Hanff
305 East 72nd Street
New York 21, New York
U.S.A.

Dear Helene,

It was good to hear from you again. Yes, we're still here, getting older and busier but no richer.

We have just managed to obtain a copy of E. M. Delafield's Diary of a Provincial Lady, in an edition published by Macmillan in 1942, a good clean copy, price $2.00. We are sending it off to you today by Book Post with invoice enclosed.

We had a very pleasant summer with more than the usual number of tourists, including hordes of young people making the pilgrimage to Carnaby Street. We watch it all from a safe distance, though I must say I rather like the Beatles. If the fans just wouldn't scream so.

Nora and the girls send their love,

Frank

September 30, 1968

Still alive, are we?

I've been writing American history books for children for four or five years. Got hung up on the stuff and have been buying American history books—in ugly, cardboardy American editions, but somehow I just didn't think the stately homes of England would yield nice English editions of James Madison's stenographic record of the Constitutional Convention or T. Jefferson's letters to J. Adams or like that.

Are you a grandfather yet? Tell Sheila and Mary their children are entitled to presentation copies of my Collected Juvenile Works, THAT should make them rush off and reproduce.

I introduced a young friend of mine to Pride & Prejudice one rainy Sunday and she has gone out of her mind for Jane Austen. She has a birthday round about Hallowe'en, can you find me some Austen for her? If you've got a complete set let me know the price, if it's expensive I'll make her husband give her half and I'll give her half.

Best to Nora and anybody else around.

Helene

MARKS & CO., Booksellers
84, Charing Cross Road
London, W.C. 2

16th October, 1968

Miss Helene Hanff
305 East 72nd Street
New York City, N.Y. 10021
U.S.A.

Dear Helene,

Yes, we are all very much alive and kicking, though rather exhausted from a hectic summer, with hordes of tourists from U.S.A., France, Scandinavia, etc., all buying our nice leather-bound books. Consequently our stock at the moment is a sorry sight, and with the shortage of books and high prices there is little hope of finding any Jane Austen for you in time for your friend's birthday. Perhaps we will be able to find them for her for Christmas.

Nora and the girls are fine. Sheila is teaching, Mary is engaged to a very nice boy but there is little hope of them getting married for some time as neither has any money! So Nora's hopes of being a glamorous grandmother are receding fast.

Love,

Frank

MARKS & CO., Booksellers
84, Charing Cross Road
London, W.C. 2

8th January, 1969

Miss H. Hanff
305 E. 72nd Street
N.Y. 10021
U.S.A.

Dear Miss,

I have just come across the letter you wrote to Mr. Doel on the 30th of September last, and it is with great regret that I have to tell you that he passed away on Sunday the 22nd of December, the funeral took place last week on Wednesday the 1st of January.

He was rushed to hospital on the 15th of December and operated on at once for a ruptured appendix, unfortunately peritonitis set in and he died seven days later.

He had been with the firm for over forty years and naturally it has come as a very great shock to Mr. Cohen, particularly coming so soon after the death of Mr. Marks.

Do you still wish us to try and obtain the Austens for you?

Yours faithfully,
p.p. MARKS & CO.

Joan Todd (*Mrs.*)
Secretary

Dear Helene,

Thank you for your very kind letter, nothing about it at all offends me. I only wish that you had met Frank and known him personally, he was the most well-adjusted person with a marvelous sense of humour, and now I realize such a modest person, as I have had letters from all over to pay him tribute and so many people in the book trade say he was so knowledgeable and imparted his knowledge with kindness to all and sundry. If you wish it I could send them to you.

At times I don't mind telling you I was very jealous of you, as Frank so enjoyed your letters and they or some were so like his sense of humour. Also I envied your writing ability. Frank and I were so very much opposites, he so kind and gentle and me with my Irish background always fighting for my rights. I miss him so, life was so interesting, he always explaining and trying to teach me something of books. My girls are wonderful and in this I am lucky. I suppose so many like me are all alone. Please excuse my scrawl.

With love,

Nora

I hope some day you will come and visit us, the girls would love to meet you.

Dear Katherine—

I take time out from housecleaning my bookshelves and sitting on the rug surrounded by books in every direction scrawl you a Bon Voyage. I hope you and Brian have a ball in London. He said to me on the phone: "Would you go with us if you had the fare?" and I nearly wept.

But I don't know, maybe it's just as well I never got there. I dreamed about it for so many years. I used to go to English movies just to look at the streets. I remember years ago a guy I knew told me that people going to England find exactly what they go looking for. I said I'd go looking for the England of English literature, and he nodded and said: "It's there."

Maybe it is, and maybe it isn't. Looking around the rug one thing's for sure: it's here.

The blessed man who sold me all my books died a few months ago. And Mr. Marks who owned the shop is dead. But Marks & Co. is still there. If you happen to pass by 84 Charing Cross Road, kiss it for me? I owe it so much.

Helene

EPILOGUE
October, 1969

October, 1969

Dear Helene,

This is correspondent No. 3 of the Doel family speaking! First, may I apologize for the long silence. Believe me, you were often in our thoughts, we just never seemed to get around to committing those thoughts to paper. And then today we got your second letter, and were so ashamed of ourselves that we're writing immediately.

We're pleased to hear about your book and very willingly give permission to publish the letters.

We are now in our lovely new home. But although we love the house, and are very happy we moved, we often think of how much my father would have enjoyed it.

It's futile to have regrets. Although my father was never a wealthy or powerful man, he was a happy and contented one. And we're happy that this was so.

We all lead busy lives—perhaps it's better so. Mary works hard at the University library, and for relaxation goes on car rallies which last all night. I'm studying part time for a degree as well as teaching full time, and Mum—she never stops! So I'm afraid we're very bad correspondents—though delighted, of course, to receive letters. Nevertheless, we will try to write when we can if you would like this, and look forward to hearing from you.

Yours truly,

Sheila

Helene Hanff has been writing letters all her life but in addition she has studied playwriting at the Theatre Guild, written for "The Hallmark Hall of Fame" and "Ellery Queen", and has been elected the first woman president of the Lenox Hill Democratic Club. She has written many books for children as well as articles for the *New Yorker* and *Harpers* magazines. Her most recent book is THE MOVERS AND SHAKERS: *The Young Activists of the Sixties.*

This book was set on the
lintotype in Monticello.
It was set, printed,
and bound at Kingsport Press, Inc.,
Kingsport, Tennessee.
Designed by Jacqueline Schuman.